The Essentials of Success:

101 Quick Questions
Every Leader Should Know

By

Joseph Morris

The Essentials of Success:
101 Quick Questions
Every Leader Should Know

Dedication

To my precious family, friends, and mentors, thank you for being an inspiration in my life. Without you, my journey to success would have been impossible. Words cannot express my deepest gratitude. I am forever grateful for your love and support.

The Essentials of Success:
101 Quick Questions
Every Leader Should Know

ISBN: 9781071455135

PRINTED IN THE UNITED STATES OF AMERICA

This Book Belongs to:

W

Table of Contents

Table of Contents

Table of Contents

Introduction

In today's complex world, trying to accomplish your personal goals can appear to be a monumental task. In fact, it may seem as if everything you do in life is challenged or requires a plausible explanation. As you strive toward achieving success there are many sacrifices to contemplate. But, in order to be victorious at whatever you do, you must have a vision and be able to walk with self-confidence. Whether it's your personal time, knowledge, or resources, if you want to be a successful leader, you must prepare yourself for the challenges ahead and be willing to commit to the journey. So exactly how do you know if you are ready to walk into your ultimate destiny? Starting with the **5-W** questions; **W**HO, **W**HAT, **W**HY, **W**HEN and **W**HERE can assist you.

I'm sure you have read several self-help books about the strategies, behaviors, and skills required for goal attainment. But unlike other novels, this book offers 101 questions that are designed to provide you with the necessary tools to guide and assess your level of self-awareness and readiness for success.

As you read each chapter, try to answer each question as thoroughly and honestly as possible. Remember this book is designed to assist you with taking a personal look at your goals and objectives by asking the right questions. There are no right or wrong answers, only room for improvement through self-reflection, so don't be critical of yourself. However, you may find that some questions will challenge you to assess and reflect on your aspirations, accomplishments, strengths, areas of improvement, and perhaps existing relationships.

During my personal journey to success, I have found that embracing the "5-W" questions have been most helpful with keeping me focused on achieving my personal goals. Therefore, I am confident that if you are able to answer the 101 queries, you too will find yourself moving toward a positive direction of self-achievement. After researching hundreds of articles, books, online media, and evaluating my own personal experiences, I think the readers will find that these tips capture the essence of success and are extremely practical for use in any setting.

Like most authors, I personally thank you for purchasing a copy of this book and sharing it with your colleagues, family members, and friends. I hope you find the information helpful and I welcome your feedback.

-Joseph Morris

The Golden Rule

The 20-questions listed throughout each chapter are part of a self-evaluation process. Also included are short exercises, case studies, a personal goal log, and reflection section to document your thoughts and feelings. Each item is designed to help you cogitate on your experiences and journey to success. As a golden rule, remember there is no right or wrong answer, only room for improvement through self-reflection and discovery. So try to answer all of the questions to the best of your ability. Have fun exploring each chapter, but most importantly, allow this book to guide your attitudes, values, and beliefs as you complete each section.

W

Chapter 1:
WHO?

"Many of life's failures are people WHO did not realize how close they were to success when they gave up."

-Thomas Edison

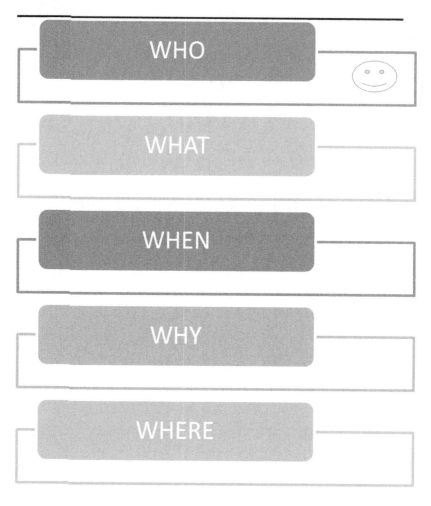

WHO

WHAT

WHEN

WHY

WHERE

"Knowing yourself is the beginning of all wisdom."

-Aristotle

WHO is perhaps the most important question that a leader can ask to gain clarity about one's defined purpose and reason for existence. The term is associated with "knowing" and becoming "enlightened" about specific facts.[1,2] Before you can answer the questions related to **WHAT, WHY, WHEN** and **WHERE** to success, you must begin with defining **WHO** you are as a person and the type of leader you desire to become. Answering the questions related to WHO will provide insight into one's character, level of confidence, and self-awareness. When this state of consciousness is achieved, the individual will be able to better understand his or her values, strengths, areas of improvement, ability to make appropriate decisions, and skills to effectively influence change. Conversely, when one is not able to answer the WHO queries, he or she may begin to doubt their abilities, goals, and feelings of self-worth. They may even start to roam aimlessly throughout life searching for answers to an unfulfilled purpose.

Seemingly, when one's purpose is not revealed, the authority to gain personal control over life's decisions can become distorted and/or dictated by other people or extenuating circumstances thus leaving the individual feeling disheartened and helpless. When one becomes powerless over their own destiny, the feelings of despair will eventually rob them of self-confidence and hope. Yet, when one is able to consciously express WHO they are; then no person, place, or thing can define their happiness or journey to success.

---

[1] https://www.dictionay.com
[2] https://www.dictionary.cambridge.com

So, in essence, the question WHO starts the voyage of self-discovery by asking, "Do you know WHO are you at the core of your being?" When one can definitively answer the questions related to WHO throughout this chapter; hopefully they will gain a better understanding of their fundamental values, goals, and purpose in life. And with an optimistic outlook, begin to soul search for the missing components of their human nature and start filling in the conscious gaps.

As a leader, be confident
in knowing WHO you
are. Be the maverick of
change and walk with
confidence!
Be loyal and true to what
you believe.
But most of all,
Love yourself above all
things!

-Joseph Morris

Please complete the following questions listed below. The spaces provided are designed for you to document three (3) responses. Remember there is no right or wrong answer. However, try to be honest and transparent as possible.

Who...

1. Are you?

    * _____

    * _____

    * _____

2. Do people say you are?

    * _____

    * _____

    * _____

3. Are your three (3) closest friends?

    * _____

    * _____

    * _____

> ## Thoughts to Consider
>
> *"The best place for self-criticism starts with you looking in front of the mirror."*
>
> *-English Proverb*

4. Motivates you to be your best?

    * _____

    * _____

    * _____

W

Who…

5. Are your mentors?
    * _____
    * _____
    * _____

6. Do you mentor?
    * _____
    * _____
    * _____

7. Do you need to forgive for any
    wrong doing?
    * _____
    * _____
    * _____

8. Do you delegate to?
    * _____
    * _____
    * _____

Thoughts to Consider

"Our goals can only be reached through a vehicle of a plan, in which we must fervently believe, and upon which we must vigorously act. There is no other route to success."

-Pablo Picasso

W

Who…

9. Are the constituents you provide service to?

    * _____
    * _____
    * _____

10. Are your foes?

    * _____
    * _____
    * _____

11. Are your role models?

    * _____
    * _____
    * _____

| Thoughts to |
| Consider |

"Never abandon your vision. Keep reaching to further your dreams."

-Benjamin Banneker

12. Do you need to distance yourself from?

    * _____
    * _____
    * _____

Remember, there are no Right or Wrong answers!

Who...

13. Do you need to establish a better personal relationship with?
    * _____
    * _____
    * _____

14. Are you personally affiliated with (top three (3) persons of influence)?
    * _____
    * _____
    * _____

> **Thoughts to Consider**
>
> *"Be yourself; everyone else is already taken."*
>
> *-Oscar Wilde*

15. Would you like to affiliate yourself with professionally (top three (3) persons of influence)?
    * _____
    * _____
    * _____

16. Do you trust enough to confide in or become vulnerable with?
    * _____
    * _____
    * _____

W

Who…

17. Are you socially connected with (top three (3) groups/person(s) of influence)?

    * _____

    * _____

    * _____

18. Holds you accountable?

    * _____

    * _____

    * _____

19. Do you hold accountable?

    * _____

    * _____

    * _____

> **Thoughts to Consider**
>
> *"He WHO knows others is wise. He WHO knows himself is enlightened."*
>
> *-Lao Tzu*

20. Challenges and/or encourages you to be great?

    * _____

    * _____

    * _____

A Case in Point: WHO's Johnny

Johnny is a 24-year-old male who spent the last five (5) years of his life hanging out with friends and living at home with his parents. He worked full-time at the local restaurant as a dishwasher and waiter. Johnny is unsure of his future plans. Although as a child he always dreamed of becoming a firefighter. For many years, he struggled with his cultural identity and being accepted into a predominately White, middle class, community.

The relationship with his step-father was extremely contentious. Unfortunately, Johnny never had the opportunity to know his biological dad, who died in an automobile collision, when he was two (2) years-old. And for many years, Johnny harbored anger and resentment toward his mother and blamed her for the reckless accident that killed his beloved father.

Johnny was often referred to as a weird and introverted kid. In fact, when hanging out with his acquaintances, he was frequently the punchline of many racial slurs and jokes. Eventually, he began to accept many of the insults as status quo and a normal way of life.

Out of all the places he has been employed, Johnny mostly enjoyed working at the local restaurant. It was a place where he could be himself without being judged and ridiculed. Until one day he received a written notice that the restaurant was closing within 30-days and that he needed to look for another place of employment. With no real plans or set goals in life, he began wandering aimlessly in search of a defined purpose and the true meaning of self-actualization.

Because of his lack of confidence, Johnny began to exhibit signs and symptoms of depression. His dearest friends have all moved on with their lives and established meaningful careers, families, and other long-lasting relationships. Meanwhile, his parents were becoming more frustrated with him living at home and increasingly co-dependent on their financial support. Not knowing what direction in life to take, Johnny began using drugs and alcohol as a way to cope and escape from reality. He eventually became a chemically dependent substance abuser and resorted to a lifestyle of panhandling and aggressive crimes to support his habits.

Unfortunately, Johnny never recovered from the addictions that robbed him of his undiscovered potential. WHO he was and WHO was to become was never achieved. The dreams of becoming a firefighter became just a figment of the imagination.

Sadly, his life ended far too soon at the age of 26. One day he was found deceased in an abandoned building as a result of a heroin drug overdose.

LIFE ALERT!

Success requires that individuals spend quality time alone reflecting on their purpose and building the confidence to embark on that purpose.

A Case in Point:
Proud Mary is WHO I Am

Mary Ann is preparing to graduate from Morris Day High-School. She recently turned seventeen and is looking forward to enrolling into her top picked university. Mary Ann or Sunshine, the nickname her friends gave her at age 7, was the captain of the cheerleading team and voted class homecoming queen. She also received a four-year academic scholarship in which she plans to major in political science.

Sunshine has a dream of one day becoming a corporate lawyer at a major law firm. With her ambition and dedication, who knows, she just may start her own private practice. In fact, during her junior and senior year of high-school, Sunshine was an active member of the debate team. During her final academic semester, the debate team placed first place in the Great State Debate, a statewide competition aimed at students interested in law and public policy.

Mary Ann is considered, by most of her colleagues, to be an honest and righteous girl. Her radiant personality and self-confidence is a reflection of the strong relationship she has with her parents and mentors. Without any doubt, she is destined for greatness. Mary Ann knows exactly WHO she is and the goals she wishes to accomplish.

Questions for Discussion:

- What do you perceive are the main take-home points for each story?

- Based on the two case scenarios you have read, can you reflect on each person's story and identify any similarities or differences?

- Do you possess any characteristics similar to the persons identified in either story? Why or Why not?

A Simple Exercise

WHO you are can be directly related to how you see yourself. Words of affirmation and encouragement can be a positive motivator for change. Try circling at least ten (10) words listed below that best describe you as a leader:

Beautiful	Tender	Thoughtful	Fabulous
Loving	Wonderful	Happy	Enthusiastic
Kind	Sensitive	Genuine	Dedicated
Special	Sympathetic	Worthy	Empowered
Great	Strong	Appreciative	Creative
Valuable	Brave	Sincere	Focused
Important	Motivated	Wonderful	Trusting
Fantastic	Positive	Terrific	Welcoming
Caring	Optimistic	Confident	Honest

Personal Goals

In the spaces provided below, list three (3) personal goals related to the question "**WHO**" that you would like to achieve within the next twelve (12) months. Evaluate your progress by checking the met or unmet boxes at the end of a four (4) month period. If you did not meet your goal(s), document your plan to reassess and accomplish your objective(s).

Date:	4 Months			
Goal	Met	Unmet	Plan	
1.				
2.				
3.				
Notes:				
Date:	8 Months			
Goal	Met	Unmet	Plan	
1.				
2.				
3.				
Notes:				
Date:	12 Months			
Goal	Met	Unmet	Plan	
1.				
2.				
3.				
Notes:				

W

Time to Reflect

Now that you have completed the questions, simple exercise, personal goals log, and read the case scenarios, please take time to reflect on the queries that you had most difficulty responding to. Self-reflection begins with you taking time to look in the mirror and acknowledge your areas of improvement and strengths. How you see yourself is how others may view you as well. If you struggled with answering three (3) or more of the questions, perhaps spending more time exploring your responses is needed. Once you have successfully answered all of the questions and documented your thoughts in the self-reflection section, please move on to the next chapter.

W

SELF-REFLECTION

_____
_____
_____
_____
_____
_____

_____
_____
_____
_____
_____
_____

_____
_____
_____
_____
_____
_____
_____

_____

SELF-REFLECTION

SELF-REFLECTION

Chapter 2:
WHAT?

"It's not WHAT you look at that Matters, It's WHAT you see."

-Henry David Thoreau

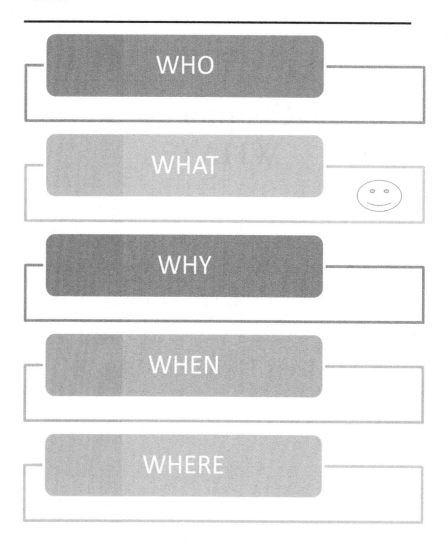

WHO

WHAT

WHY

WHEN

WHERE

"Imagination is the beginning of creation. You imagine WHAT you desire, you will WHAT you imagine and at least you create WHAT you will."

-George Bernard Shaw

WHAT is a question that is commonly used to identify a person, place, or specific thing. The question can also be used to inquire about something an individual is not accustomed to or familiar with.[3] It is the query that is adopted to fill in knowledge gaps, embrace uncertainties, or to bring about awareness (i.e. for WHAT purpose?).[4] The question also seeks factual knowledge in search of meaning and to gain a conscious understanding.

"WHAT" gives rise to the deliverables that are measurable and used to uncover the mysteries in life. The answer(s) to the question(s) is/are often attained through lived experiences, mindfulness, and emotional-intelligence. As a leader, once you are clear about the WHAT; you can better articulate your vision and defined purpose. You can take action on the things you wish to accomplish and begin to move toward your defined destiny.

Keep in mind, WHAT you "do" on your journey to success matters more than WHAT you "say" you are going to do. For example, there are many people that complain about losing weight, but when asked, "WHAT are you going to do about it?" their responses will either demonstrate the need to take action or continue to accept the same activities of daily living.

---

[3] https://www.marriam-webster.com
[4] https://www.dictionary.com

W

As you reflect on your past, present, and future plans, try to focus on the things that are most important to you. WHAT are the lessons learned, and WHAT are the goals left to be accomplished? Everyone has the potential to be a great leader however, not everyone will do WHAT it takes to be successful. Only **YOU** can define your destiny. And defining your destiny means you must be able to express WHAT it is you are trying to accomplish and willingness to do in order to make your dreams become a reality.

WHAT I've come to believe is WHAT you accept in your heart as the truth, could eventually become your reality.

-Joseph Morris

Please complete the following questions listed below. The spaces provided are designed for you to document three (3) responses. Remember there is no right or wrong answer. However, try to be honest and transparent as possible.

WHAT...

21. Is your purpose?
    * _____
    * _____
    * _____

| Thoughts to |
| Consider |

"Happiness is WHEN WHAT you think, WHAT you say, and WHAT you do are in harmony."

-Mahatma Gandhi

22. Are your professional goals?
    * _____
    * _____
    * _____

23. Are your personal goals?
    * _____
    * _____
    * _____

24. Are the things that upset you the most?
    * _____
    * _____
    * _____

W

WHAT...

25. Are the things in your life that bring you joy?
    * _____
    * _____
    * _____

26. Talents do you possess?
    * _____
    * _____
    * _____

27. Is your leadership style?
    * _____
    * _____
    * _____

> ### Thoughts to Consider
>
> *"The measure of a man is WHAT he does with the power he possesses."*
>
> *-Greek Proverb*

28. Causes you to procrastinate?
    * _____
    * _____
    * _____

WHAT...

29. Are the gaps in your leadership skills that need to be refined?

    * _____
    * _____
    * _____

30. Are your preferred communication outlets/styles?

    * _____
    * _____
    * _____

31. Are your personal strengths?

    * _____
    * _____
    * _____

32. Are your areas of improvement?

    * _____
    * _____
    * _____

> **Thoughts to Consider**
>
> *"I never could have done WHAT I have done without the habits of punctuality, order, and diligence, without the determination to concentrate myself on one subject at a time."*
>
> *-Charles Dickens*

WHAT...

33. Are your favorite hobbies?

   * _____
   * _____
   * _____

Thoughts to Consider

"Success depends on previous preparation, and without such preparation there is sure to be failure."

-Confucius

---

34. Social groups do you belong to?

   * _____
   * _____
   * _____

35. Are your spiritual beliefs?

   * _____
   * _____
   * _____

36. Are your levels of education/training?

   * _____
   * _____
   * _____

WHAT…

37. Are the professional certificates you possess?
    * _____
    * _____
    * _____

38. Are the three (3) past jobs you enjoyed working at the most?
    * _____
    * _____
    * _____

39. Motivates you to be your best?
    * _____
    * _____
    * _____

40. Discourages you from being your best?
    * _____
    * _____
    * _____

> ### Thoughts to Consider
>
> *"Make the best use of WHAT's in your power and take the rest as it happens."*
>
> *-Epictetus*

A Case in Point: WHAT the Fuss (WTF)

Jennifer is a 33-year-old female, married with two (2) children. She has spent the past ten (10) years of her life enjoying the pleasures of being a housewife and remaining actively involved with her children's afterschool activities (i.e. girls scouts, pee-wee baseball, soccer, etc.). In addition, she volunteers at the local church as a youth outreach minister while co-chairing a women's social book club. People familiar with Jennifer would describe her as a loving, pleasant, and giving person. She is extremely confident; yet, humble and caring.

Jennifer and Bob have been married for eleven (11) years. Although things may appear to be jovial on the surface, WHAT is not apparent is their disruptive relationship. Over the past year, Bob has become verbally and physically abusive. His behavior was also accompanied by excessive alcohol misuse and gambling. Unfortunately, the drinking and spending had gotten so out-of-control that the couple received several eviction and shutoff notices for not paying their apartment rent and utilities on time. Not to mention, the two felony charges Bob received while driving a motor-vehicle while

W

intoxicated, has put a severe strain on the family's transportation means. Reflecting on their vows to love each other through the good and bad times, the couple decided to seek marital counseling. And after the 5th therapy session, it was discovered that Bob was secretly having an extramarital affair and filed for a divorce.

While going through the legal process, Jennifer began to frequently ask the questions related to, "WHAT". Exactly, WHAT could she have done differently to change the outcomes of their marriage? WHAT did she do wrong? WHAT if she could rewind the hands of time and make things better? WHAT would her family and friends think of her being a single parent? and WHAT will she do to financially to survive?

Each day became more difficult for Jennifer to cope. Eventually, she started blaming herself for the failed relationship and other personal matters of concern. Her intense feelings of anger, guilt, and shame would vacillate frequently as if she was on an emotional roller coaster. Expressive outbursts were unpredictable and began to negatively impact her children's health and safety as well. Bethany, Jennifer's best friend, suggested that she and the children seek out a licensed marriage & family therapist (LMFT) to help them deal with the tumultuous family breakup.

As one year passed by and the divorce became final, Jennifer began to search for clarity regarding the WHAT in her life. Although she had enjoyed being a housewife for many years, she stopped dreaming about her future plans to one day become a Pediatric Registered Nurse.

Once Jennifer become empowered and able to clearly define her goals and objectives; she enrolled into a nursing program and ultimately graduated with top academic honors. It became apparent that discovering the WHAT in her life was missing and needed to be well-defined. Discerning the WHAT also helped her to create a personal mission statement, strategic plan, and lifetime goals. Jennifer eventually remarried and started a non-profit organization that inspires women to become self-sufficient by employing "The Essentials of Success: 101...."

A Case in Point:
Now WHAT are We to Do?

Have you ever dreamed of becoming successful and your plans were perfectly mapped out as to how you were going to get there? You even spent many years training, preparing, and discussing the details as if your survival depended on it. However, your life took a different direction from which you planned and now your initial goals needed to be redefined. Well, you are not alone. The same situation was true for Sarah and Jennifer, two best friends forever (i.e. BFFs or Besties) who considered themselves as soul sisters. They have known each other since preschool and vowed to never grow apart. In fact, they even went to the same elementary, high-school, and junior college. Sarah and Jennifer married hardworking men that loved them dearly. And just when you think you've heard it all, they both moved into the same neighborhood and birthed two beautiful children, six months apart.

Life was wonderful for the both of them, not a single life stressor. Until one early Monday morning, Jennifer received a disturbing call from Greg, her husband, regarding his employment status. Unfortunately, Greg was laid off from work and needed to look for another job. The company he had worked for more than twenty years was downsizing in order to save costs. Since Greg was one of the highest paid managers with company seniority, he was the first person to be released permanently from the organization. And to complicate matters, Jennifer received a letter from their mortgage lender stating that their monthly house payment was scheduled to increase by ten percent within the next 30-days.

With the cost of living expenses increasing and Greg being unemployed, the couple was forced to live off high interest rate loans, credit cards, and personal savings. Jennifer even obtained a part-time job to help support the family until Greg was able to secure a new place of employment. After six months of searching for full-time work, Greg eventually obtained a position at a local factory as a sales manager. Although they lost their beautiful dream home, Jennifer and Greg never lost the faith and love for each other. The couple soon relocated to a different neighborhood and reestablished their future goals. They did WHAT was necessary in order to survive, prosper, and secure their family's future.

LIFE ALERT!

Find your happy space in life. Own it and live it to the fullest!

W

Questions for Discussion:

- Based on the two scenarios, WHAT would you consider the main take home points?

- Can you identify any similarities and/or differences in each person's story?

- Have you faced similar circumstances or know someone that has? If so, WHAT was the outcome and how was the situation handled?

A Simple Exercise

Do you have exactly W.H.A.T it takes to be
a successful leader?

Willpower, **H**ope, **A**ttitude, and **T**enacity

Similar to the abbreviation above, can you create five (5) or more acronyms using the word W.H.A.T that can serve as your daily personal creed?

1._____   6._____

2._____   7._____

3._____   8._____

4._____   9._____

5._____   10._____

Personal Goals

In the spaces provided below, list three (3) personal goals related the question "**WHAT**" that you would like to achieve within the next twelve (12) months. Evaluate your progress by checking the met or unmet boxes at the end of a four (4) month period. If you did not meet your goal(s), document your plan to reassess and accomplish your objective(s).

Date:	4 Months			
Goal	Met	Unmet	Plan	
1.				
2.				
3.				
Notes:				
Date:	8 Months			
Goal	Met	Unmet	Plan	
1.				
2.				
3.				
Notes:				
Date:	12 Months			
Goal	Met	Unmet	Plan	
1.				
2.				
3.				
Notes:				

W

Time to Reflect

Now that you have completed the questions, simple exercise, personal goals log, and read the case scenarios, please take time to reflect on the queries that you had most difficulty responding to. Self-reflection begins with you taking time to look in the mirror and acknowledge your areas of improvement and strengths. How you see yourself is how others may view you as well. If you struggled with answering three (3) or more of the questions, perhaps spending more time exploring your responses is needed. Once you have successfully answered all of the questions and documented your thoughts in the self-reflection section, please move on to the next chapter.

W

SELF-REFLECTION

SELF-REFLECTION

SELF-REFLECTION

Chapter 3:
WHEN?

"WHEN one door closes another door opens; but we often look so long and so regretfully upon the closed door. That we do not see the ones which open for us."

-Alexander Graham Bell

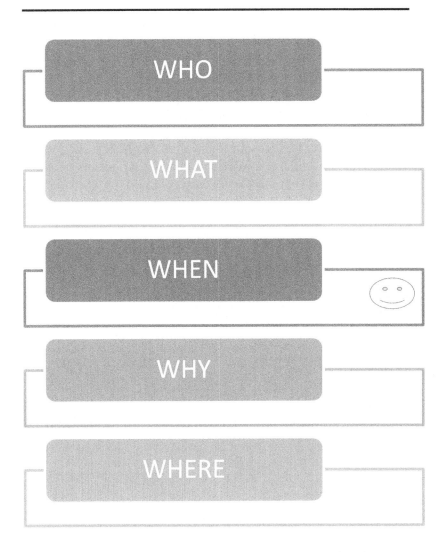

"WHEN you get to the top of the mountain, don't stop there, keep on climbing."

-Zen Proverb

W HEN, is a measurement of time that is used to account for particular events. The question "WHEN" also refers to an action that has taken place or should occur at a certain period.[5] If one has no concept of time, then the queries associated with WHEN cannot be objectively quantified. How one manages time is associated with their understanding of WHEN. Great leaders must be able to measure and manage the WHEN if they want change to take place. WHEN change is necessary with respect to time, five (5) key factors should be considered; planning, delegating, evaluating, organizing and prioritizing.[6,7,8]

[5] https://www.marriam-webster.com
[6] https://www.measureevaluation.org
[7] https://www.conovercompany.com
[8] https://www.ropella.com/ee_uploads/pub_articles/12-125.pdf

Each of these factors can have a profound effect on WHEN an assignment is accomplished. For example, if one fails to "plan" accordingly to complete a specific task, knowing exactly WHEN the job will be finished would remain questionable and difficult to accurately measure.

Once you have identified those things in your life that can directly influence either of the aforementioned factors, it is then time for you to begin working on goal attainment. However, in order to be successful, you must be willing to carve out quality time to do the work that is required. But, too often the unanswered question is..........WHEN?

Nowadays, it appears that everyone is so busy doing WHO knows WHAT that they forget WHEN to focus on taking the appropriate actions to move them closer to actualizing their dreams. If you want change to take place in your life, don't wait until tomorrow, start today! Change is sparked by having a vision. Yet, it is only WHEN the vision is clearly defined and infused with action will the power of influence be released. As a leader, you can begin taking control of your destiny by dedicating at least 30-45 minutes a day focusing on the most important person, YOU!

During your quest toward goal attainment, there will always be persons that despise your efforts (i.e. the haters). Like thieves in the night, they seek to rob you of your hopes and dreams. So never mind what they think or say about you. More than likely, they are not happy with themselves and/or suffer from long-term emptiness. Stay focused and self-centered on accomplishing your goals. Don't become easily distracted by gossip, rumors, or other frivolous things that don't encourage your success. Successful leaders know that it's okay to be selfish WHEN it comes to carving a particular niche. Remember, you are the captain of your ship and therefore set the course of direction.

Now keep in mind, at some point in time, you may become unmotivated, discouraged, and/or even redirected from your initial goals. Let's face it, life is often unpredictable, but don't give up the fight. You are designed to be more than just a conqueror. You were created with a purpose and to be victorious. Everyone has good and bad days. Yet, the race to success is not given to the fastest or strongest, but to the one that can endure the test of time.

Throughout your journey, make time for "You" by investing in yourself. Successful people spend quality time perfecting their skills, defining and refining goals, while striving for greatness.

Please complete the following questions listed below. The spaces provided are designed for you to document three (3) responses. Remember there is no right or wrong answer. However, try to be honest and transparent as possible.

WHEN...

41. Was the last time you took a personal vacation?

   * _____
   * _____
   * _____

42. Are you most productive?

   * _____
   * _____
   * _____

43. Do you find balance between work and play?

   * _____
   * _____
   * _____

> ### Thoughts to Consider
>
> *"Falling down is not a failure. Failure comes WHEN you stay WHERE you have fallen."*
>
> *-Socrates*

44. Do you meet with your mentor(s)?

   * _____
   * _____
   * _____

WHEN...

45. Do you meet with your mentee(s)?
    * _____
    * _____
    * _____

46. Do you spend quality time alone?
    * _____
    * _____
    * _____

47. Do you spend quality time with family members?
    * _____
    * _____
    * _____

48. Do you spend quality time with friends?
    * _____
    * _____
    * _____

> **Thoughts to Consider**
>
> *"Be not afraid of greatness; some are born great, some achieve greatness, and some have greatness thrust upon them."*
>
> *-William Shakespeare*

WHEN…

49. Do you engage in hobbies/fun activities of interest?

* _____

* _____

* _____

50. Do you schedule time to exercise?

* _____

* _____

* _____

51. Do you schedule time to eat a well-balanced diet?

* _____

* _____

* _____

> ## Thoughts to Consider
>
> *"If your actions inspire others to dream more, learn more, do more, and become more, you are a leader."*
>
> *-John Quincy Adams*

52. Do you schedule time to get 6-8 hours of sleep?

* _____

* _____

* _____

WHEN...

53. Do you meditate/pray?

* _____
* _____
* _____

54. Do you schedule budget planning?

* _____
* _____
* _____

55. Do you work on the gaps in your skills?

* _____
* _____
* _____

56. Do you work on the areas of self-improvement?

* _____
* _____
* _____

Thoughts to Consider

"Apply yourself both now and in the next life. Without effort, you cannot be prosperous. Through the land be good, you cannot have an abundant crop without cultivation."

-Plato

WHEN…

57. Do you evaluate your personal goals?

   * _____

   * _____

   * _____

58. Do you evaluate your professional goals?

   * _____

   * _____

   * _____

59. Do you engage in community service?

   * _____

   * _____

   * _____

60. Do you engage in the things that motivate you?

   * _____

   * _____

   * _____

> ### Thoughts to Consider
>
> *"It is not the style of clothes one wears, neither the kind of automobile one drives, nor the amount of money one has in the bank, that counts. These mean nothing. It is simply service that measures success."*
>
> *-George Washington Carver*

A Case in Point:
WHEN the Time is Right

Tracy is a 24-year-old female that works as an administrative assistant for a small non-profit corporation. She has three siblings, ages 7, 12, and 17. For the past 25-years, her parents have labored as farm workers to support the family with great hopes of retiring within five (5) years. Unfortunately, a recent change in their health conditions has caused an alteration in plans. Tracy's mother suffered a severe stroke while working on the farm, which left her permanently paralyzed and unable to ambulate independently. And to complicate matters, she recently learned that her father is now suffering from the early stages of dementia and no longer able to make logical decisions.

Tracy's father has always been sympathetic of her working to help support the household; however, he strongly encourages education as the gateway to financial independence. With the hopes of living the American dream, she enrolled in online courses at a local community college with plans to complete an associate degree in business. Tracy's dream is to one day obtain a Master's in Business

W

Administration (MBA) degree and own a successful investment firm. With only seven months left until graduation, she will be the first person in her family to graduate from college.

Over the past several months her family has faced extreme financial hardships. Unfortunately, Tracy is barely able to afford food, living expenses, and medical expenditures. Her 17-year old brother has even offered to drop out of high-school in order to assist with caregiver duties. However, Tracy insisted that he stay focused on maintaining good academic grades and providing support with raising their younger siblings.

Forced to make a tough decision, does she work more hours to support the household, or instead, focus on graduating from college with the hopes of landing a better paying job; Tracy decided to stay on track and complete the graduation requirements. Hoping one day she will be able to afford the assistance needed to provide optimal care for her parents and acquire a better lifestyle for the entire family.

Faith and time were critical factors in Tracy's decision-making process. The burdens she carried seemed too difficult to bear and hope was fading fast. There were many days she felt like having a mental meltdown. However, she persevered and eventually graduated from a community college before transferring to a University to complete the

W

MBA requirements. Not too soon after obtaining her degree, Tracy was offered a leadership position at a banking institution. Still motivated for change, within a year's time, she started an online business which grossed over $200,000. In fact, the company thrived so well that she was able to afford the healthcare services and lifestyle she always dreamed of having.

LIFE ALERT!

Life is not so rigid. It's full of twists and turns. So be flexible and change with it.

W

A Case in Point: I Remember WHEN

After a long eight hours day of work, Samson likes to work out at the gym for 30-minutes before heading home. He has always been very prideful about his appearance; taking his exercise regimen very seriously. Surprisingly, most people do not know that Samson was extremely obese at one point. At a height of five feet, seven inches, and a previous weight of four hundred (400) pounds, he had many hazards to his health. His primary physician warned him about the risk of having a massive stroke, heart attack, and other health complications. Considering he has a family history of cardiovascular disease and co-morbid conditions, the health warnings were enough to stimulate the need for change in his sedentary lifestyle.

Samson is a proud military veteran; having served ten years in active duty before being honorably discharged. His initial goal was to remain enlisted with the hopes of retiring as a high ranking official. Unfortunately, during a routine military training, he suffered multiple injuries to his lower extremities from an accidental fall.

W

As a result, Samson required a below-the-knee amputation of his left leg which left him permanently disabled. For the remainder of his life, he would require a prosthetic limb to ambulate. Unfortunately, this manner of living began to impact his psychosocial well-being. He eventually became depressed and threatened suicide on multiple occasions. In order to cope with having a physical impairment he often found comfort in the gluttony of food and engaging in other non-healthy activities. This lifestyle was much different from the values he learned from his military training.

After receiving intense mental and physical therapy, Samson began to feel hopeful about the future. Although he suffered a life changing injury, he did not allow the disability to interfere with his pursuit of happiness. He enrolled in an automotive training program at a local college. Two years later, he graduated with an associate degree in small engine repair and eventually opened up an automotive shop. Within six months, the business became so lucrative that he was able to expand the operations into two different locations.

Questions for Discussion:

- Based on the two case studies you have read, can you reflect on each person's story and identify any similarities or differences?

- How would you describe their personalities based on the information provided?

- Do you possess any characteristics similar to the persons identified in the story? Why or Why not?

A Simple Exercise

Try completing the following statements below. After you have filled in all of the blanks, take a moment to identify any areas of personal need or improvement based on the responses you provided?

WHEN I turned age _____, I first learned how to _____. However, it wasn't until I turned _____, I began to_____. WHEN thinking about the choices that I have made in my life, I often wish I would have_____ more. In fact, WHEN everyone was busy _____ I was preoccupied with _____. However, now that I am older and more experienced, WHEN the time is right I will focus more on _____. Even WHEN I have given it my best attempt and all has failed, I will continue to _____. For I hold the keys to my destiny even WHEN I am challenged and feel like giving up. WHEN I am feeling sad and depressed I will_____ to cheer me up. WHEN I need a shoulder to lean on I will call on_____, _____, or even _____ to help me get through the rough times.

W

Personal Goals

In the spaces provided below, list three (3) personal goals related to the question "**WHEN**" that you would like to achieve within the next twelve (12) months. Evaluate your progress by checking the met or unmet boxes at the end of a four (4) month period. If you did not meet your goal(s), document your plan to reassess and accomplish your objective(s).

Date:	4 Months		
Goal	Met	Unmet	Plan
1.			
2.			
3.			
Notes:			
Date:	8 Months		
Goal	Met	Unmet	Plan
1.			
2.			
3.			
Notes:			
Date:	12 Months		
Goal	Met	Unmet	Plan
1.			
2.			
3.			
Notes:			

W

Time to Reflect

Now that you have completed the questions, simple exercise, personal goals log, and read the case scenarios, please take time to reflect on the queries that you had most difficulty responding to. Self-reflection begins with you taking time to look in the mirror and acknowledge your areas of strengths and improvement. If you struggled with answering three (3) or more of the questions, perhaps spending more time exploring your responses is needed. Once you have successfully answered all of the questions and documented your thoughts in the self-reflection section, please move on to the next chapter.

SELF-REFLECTION

_____

_____

_____

_____

_____

_____

_____

_____

_____

_____

_____

_____

_____

_____

_____

_____

_____

SELF-REFLECTION

SELF-REFLECTION

Chapter 4:
WHY?

"Strive for that greatness of spirit that measures life not by its disappointments but by its possibilities."

-W.E.B. Dubois

WHO

WHAT

WHEN

WHY

WHERE

"Live your life while you have it. Life is a splendid gift-there is nothing small in it."

-Florence Nightingale

WHY is the question that is commonly asked to seek clarity or justification for carrying out certain actions.[9] It attempts to provide plausible answers to queries and actions with logical reason. WHY helps explain WHAT one plans to accomplish as related to specific goals and objectives. Leaders must be able to define the "WHY" and capable of articulating the reasons for doing WHAT they do with precision and purpose.

When one is not able to explain "WHY" or provide an explanation as to the reason he or she is performing a particular task, then those individuals may be at risk for lacking the critical thinking skills necessary to make appropriate decisions. In addition, when there are knowledgeable gaps in understanding WHY, it is easy for a person to become more task-oriented and driven only by outcomes rather than focusing on the purpose and need for change.

Great leaders, who are able to explain WHY they are performing certain tasks, are confident enough to predict outcomes and set new direction if needed.[10,11]   Therefore, explaining the "WHY perhaps the second most important question for self-discovery. The rationale provided to this query

[9] https://www.dictionary.cambridge.com
[10] https: //www.intelliven.com/how-to-set-direction-when-the-leader-is-not-sure-about-where-to-head-next/
[11] https://www.inc.com/resources/leadership/articles/20080301/dao.html

W

could potentially differentiate the "novice" learner from the "expert."

Every great new innovation that mankind has ever revealed has been challenged by trying to clarify WHY. WHY it is important, WHY it will make a difference, or even WHY anyone would even care. Out of all the questions you may be faced with as a leader, being able to provide a rationale to justify WHY an action was taken or a decision made will foster greater respect, loyalty, and trust amongst your peers and supporters.[12,13] No matter WHO you are or WHAT you do, if you can't explain the WHY, then you want have a clear understanding of your motivations.

> If you are unsure as to WHY you are doing what you do, don't be afraid to seek clarity.
>
> -Joseph Morris

---

[12] https://www.thriveglobal.com
[13] https://www. amanet.org/articles/how-to-use-communication-to-build-trust-and-inspire-loyalty-as-well-as-lead-effectively/

Please complete the following questions listed below. The spaces provided are designed for you to document three (3) responses. Remember there is no right or wrong answer. However, try to be honest and transparent as possible.

WHY...

61. Do you like your job and/or profession?

* _____

* _____

* _____

62. Do you associate with the three (3) friends you previously listed?

* _____

* _____

* _____

63. Did you select the mentor(s) you previously identified?

* _____

* _____

* _____

64. Do you want to be a mentor?

* _____

* _____

* _____

> ## Thoughts to Consider
>
> *"All highly competent people continually search for ways to keep learning, growing, and improving. They do that by asking WHY. After all, the person who knows how will always have a job, but the person WHO knows WHY will always be the boss."*
>
> *-Benjamin Franklin*

WHY...

65. Do you need to be affiliated with a professional group/organization?

    * _____

    * _____

    * _____

Thoughts to Consider

66. Do you need to spend time alone?

    * _____

    * _____

    * _____

"Keep your face toward the sunshine and shadows will fall behind you."

67. Do you mediate/pray?

    * _____

    * _____

    * _____

-Walt Whitman

68. Do you engage in community service?

    * _____

    * _____

    * _____

WHY…

69. Do you need to exercise?

    * _____
    * _____
    * _____

70. Do you select the type of
    diet/foods you eat?

    * _____
    * _____
    * _____

71. Do you sleep during the times you
    previously stated?

    * _____
    * _____
    * _____

72. Do you need to forgive the
    persons you previously identified
    in question #7?

    * _____
    * _____
    * _____

> ## Thoughts to Consider
>
> *"Success is to be measured not so much by the position that one has reached in life as by the obstacles which he as overcome."*
>
> *-Booker T. Washington*

W

WHY...

73. Do you need to establish better personal relationships?

* _____
* _____
* _____

74. Are you personally affiliated with the persons you previously identified?

* _____
* _____
* _____

75. Would you like to professionally affiliate yourself with the organization(s) you previously identified?

* _____
* _____
* _____

> ### Thoughts to Consider
>
> *"If you want to succeed you should strike out new paths rather than travel the worn paths of accepted success."*
>
> *-John D. Rockefeller*

76. Do you need to work on the areas of improvement you previously mentioned?

* _____
* _____
* _____

WHY...

77. Do you need to work on gaps in your leadership skills you previously mentioned?
    * _____
    * _____
    * _____

Thoughts to Consider

"Our greatest weakness lies in giving up. The most certain way to succeed is to always try just one more time."

-Thomas Edison

---

78. Do you need to revisit your personal goals?
    * _____
    * _____
    * _____

79. Do you need to revisit your professional goals?
    * _____
    * _____
    * _____

80. Did you select the management style you previously mentioned?
    * _____
    * _____
    * _____

LIFE ALERT!

Only you hold the key
to unlock your destiny!

"I had to make my own living and my
own opportunity. But I made it!
Don't sit down and wait for the
opportunity to come. Get up and
make them."

-Madam C.J. Walker

W

A Case in Point
WHY Ask WHY:

Have you ever asked the question WHY certain things happen that appear to have no rationale or apparent justification?   For example, WHY must innocent people die over religious beliefs or WHY did someone get a promotion over you when they are seemingly the least qualified?   Or perhaps, WHY is the price of gas steadily rising when there are more hybrid cars being manufactured?

WHY is the most frequent question that is asked for the inquisitive mind.   Let's take for example, Abdul Mohammed, who posted the question on social media, "WHY must society prejudge persons of the Islamic faith, as if to say all Muslims are terrorists, when in fact the religion teaches principles of love and peace?   And just because an individual may dress or speak with a dialect that is different from the popular culture, it does not mean they are less knowledgeable,   incompetent,   or   pose   an environmental threat."

For the past two (2) years, Mark has frequently seen Abdul shopping at the local grocery store.   Abdul has always made it a priority to acknowledge Mark by saying, "hello" or "have a wonderful day."

However, Mark has never returned the gesture in kind. Instead, he would whisper remarks to the store security guard such as, "I think you should watch that suspicious man closely........" Unknowingly, Mark would one day meet face-to-face with Abdul in a place where frequently life and death are placed in the hands of complete strangers.

For more than fifteen years, Dr. Abdul Mohammed has worked as the Chief Pediatric Surgeon at the local County Hospital. He is nationally recognized for his passion for children and superb surgical skills. Not to mention, his dedication and kindness for all patients has earned him the National Medical Doctor of the Year Award. Nevertheless, it was a hot summer day when Mark's five year old son, Jacob, was riding his bike in the neighborhood and was hit by a speeding driver. First responders were notified and Jacob was rushed to the emergency room.

Immediately upon admission, it was noted that Jacob had suffered from several broken bones, a concussion, and therefore needed an urgent operation. The Surgeon on call that evening was none other than Dr. Abdul Mohammed. Once he had heard of the tragic situation, he immediately instructed the surgical team to prepare for an emergency operation. While preparing for Jacob's operation, Dr. Mohammed walked into the waiting room to meet with the nervously awaiting parents. Surprisingly there was Mark standing with tears in his eyes as he looked at the renowned surgeon with pure conviction and remorse. Without any fear or hesitation, Dr. Mohammed embraced Mark and ensured him that he will take great care of Jacob and provide frequent updates. After four hours of operation, the procedure went well and Jacob was on his way to a successful recovery. The only thing left to explore was Mark's previous perceptions, feelings and answers to the question.....WHY?

A Case in Point
WHY Not Now:

Sometimes we can begin our journey to success with great ideas and expectations, but often life has a way of throwing you a curve ball, which forces you to reevaluate your plans. No matter how skilled or intelligent you are, no one is perfect. As humans, we are all capable of failure. Everyone has limitations; even the most gifted person is subject to face the agony of defeat. However, leaders that are resilient and motivated to change are able to withstand the challenges of life no matter the circumstances.

Such is the case of David, a 34-year-old male who spent the past decade working his way up the corporate ladder with the hopes of becoming a supervisor or executive manager. David was the ideal employee. He hardly missed any days of work and was extremely committed to supporting the company's mission. He was honest, hardworking, and respected by his fellow colleagues. Although he met all of the qualifying benchmarks to become a manager, he was missing the necessary trainings that were required to oversee the daily operations of a large corporation.

Therefore, David sought out mentors for support and guidance to ensure he was taking the proper steps that would lead to his success. He even developed a personal mission statement and began to map out a two-year plan to obtain the job he envisioned. Over the past several years he remained focused and motivated. David accomplished each goal and completed every milestone his mentors recommended.

Soon came the day for him to actualize his dreams; a job was posted for the leadership role he so patiently trained and waited for. With much anticipation, he applied and interviewed for the management position. The selection process was extremely competitive. However, David was confident that he would be selected for the job. After much anticipation and waiting for two weeks, he received a letter in the mail stating, "We regret to inform you that you were not selected for the position....." Initially, David was shocked and disappointed he did not receive the job of his dreams. But instead of being angry and feeling sorry for himself, he continued to persevere and seek out learning experiences that would strengthen his profile as a potential candidate for a leadership role.

After several unsuccessful interviews, he was eventually hired into a management position. All of his efforts were not in vain. After a year had passed, David received the organization's Manager of the Year award. This acknowledgment is given to an individual that shows exemplary leadership skills. Although the road to success was paved with several setbacks and disappointments, David never gave up on his dreams.

Questions for Discussion:

- Based on the two case studies you have read, can you reflect on each person's story and identify any similarities or differences?

- Do you possess any characteristics similar to the persons identified in the story? Why or Why not?

- What do you perceive are the main take-home points for each story?

A Simple Exercise

In general, the answers to the questions associated with WHY will separate the beginning learner from someone WHO is more experienced. Using the space provided below, can you describe WHY do you need to be Successful? And WHY it is important for you to be a Great Leader?

<u>Successful</u>   <u>Great Leader</u>

1. ._____   1. ._____

2. ._____   2. ._____

3. ._____   3. ._____

4. ._____   4. ._____

5. ._____   5. ._____

Personal Goals

In the spaces provided below, list three (3) personal goals related the question "**WHY**" that you would like to achieve within the next twelve (12) months. Evaluate your progress by checking the met or unmet boxes at the end of a four (4) month period. If you did not meet your goal(s), document your plan to reassess and accomplish your objective(s).

Date:	4 Months		
Goal	Met	Unmet	Plan
1.			
2.			
3.			
Notes:			
Date:	8 Months		
Goal	Met	Unmet	Plan
1.			
2.			
3.			
Notes:			
Date:	12 Months		
Goal	Met	Unmet	Plan
1.			
2.			
3.			
Notes:			

Time to Reflect

Now that you have completed the questions, simple exercise, personal goals log, and read the case scenarios, please take time to reflect on the queries that you had most difficulty responding to. Self-reflection begins with you taking time to look in the mirror and acknowledge your areas of improvement and strengths. If you struggled with answering three (3) or more of the questions, perhaps spending more time exploring your responses is needed. Once you have successfully answered all of the questions and documented your thoughts in the self-reflection section, please move on to the next chapter.

SELF-REFLECTION

SELF-REFLECTION

SELF-REFLECTION

_____

_____

_____

_____

_____

_____

_____

_____

_____

_____

_____

_____

_____

_____

_____

_____

_____

_____

_____

_____

_____

_____

Chapter 5:
WHERE?

"Do not go WHERE the path may lead, go instead WHERE there is no path and leave a trail."

-Ralph Waldo Emerson

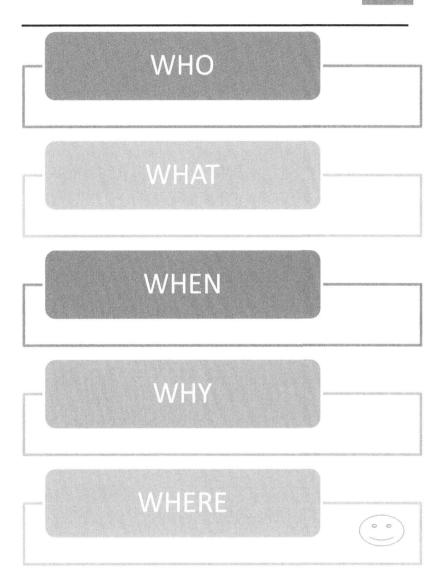

"If you desire to be a great leader in life, must be willing to be a bridge."

-Welsh Proverb

WHERE, is the question that usually refers to a particular place or a point in time at which something happened or will take place[14]. In addition, it may reference a certain destination or position. For example, WHERE you see yourself in "x" number or years is perhaps the most common question an employer would ask an interviewee. Although you may or may not know the exact answer, the query is aimed to solicit a response regarding one's personal goals and/or qualification.[15]

Everyone has personal and professional goals, however understanding WHERE you are positioned in life can reflect your level of stability, ambition, and interest. Throughout your journey to success, you should spend quality time taking inventory of past experiences and personal goals. Life as you may know it today is not guaranteed. WHERE you are currently situated may not be WHERE you ultimately end up.

Life has a funny way of taking many unexpected turns. However, success is a process; it takes time to perfect, and does not always come easy. During your quest for personal achievement, make sure you

[14] https://www.merriam-webster.com

[15] https://www.themuse.com/advice/how-to-answer-where-do-you-see-yourself-in-5-years

are doing WHAT makes you happy. Be the best at WHAT you do and find comfort in your desires. However, don't rest your happiness on the grounds of material things. They will only bring you temporary satisfaction. Success is not defined by the amount of money you have, educational degrees, or the position you obtain. Yet, it is ultimately measured by the level of personal fulfillment and self-gratification.

Every great leader has a starting point in their journey to success. However, WHERE they end up in life is often a result of great preparation, planning, and decision making.

-Joseph Morris

Please complete the following questions listed below. The spaces provided are designed for you to document three (3) responses. Remember there is no right or wrong answer. However, try to be honest and transparent as possible.

WHERE...

81. Do you prefer to spend quality time alone?
    * _____
    * _____
    * _____

82. Do you spend quality time with family?
    * _____
    * _____
    * _____

83. Do you spend quality time with friends?
    * _____
    * _____
    * _____

84. Do you spend time volunteering for community service?
    * _____
    * _____
    * _____

> ### Thoughts to Consider
>
> *"Let me tell you the secret that has led me to my goal. My strength lies solely in my tenacity."*
>
> *-Louis Pasteur*

W

WHERE…

85. Do you spend your time exercising?

* _____
* _____
* _____

86. Do you spend most of your time eating?

* _____
* _____
* _____

87. Do you spend most of your time socializing?

* _____
* _____
* _____

> ### Thoughts to Consider
>
> *"If you don't change the direction, you may end up WHERE you are going."*
>
> -Lao Tzu

88. Do you commonly meet with your mentor(s)?

* _____
* _____
* _____

W

WHERE...

89. Do you commonly meet with your mentee(s)?
    * _____
    * _____
    * _____

90. Do you meet with your confidants?
    * _____
    * _____
    * _____

> **Thoughts to Consider**
>
> *"WHERE the needs of the world are and your talents cross, there lies your vocation."*
>
> *-Aristotle*

91. Do you demonstrate your talents/skills?
    * _____
    * _____
    * _____

92. Do you frequently seek education/knowledge?
    * _____
    * _____
    * _____

WHERE…

93. Do you do your best planning?
    * _____
    * _____
    * _____

94. Where (location) do you spend your time sleeping?
    * _____
    * _____
    * _____

95. Where did you complete your educational training?
    * _____
    * _____
    * _____

> ## Thoughts to Consider
>
> *"The key to success is action, and the essential in action is perseverance."*
>
> *-Sun Yat-sen*

96. Where do you practice your spiritual/meditation rituals?
    * _____
    * _____
    * _____

WHERE...

97. Do you exercise your leadership skills?
    * _____
    * _____
    * _____

98. Do you exercise your
    management skills?
    * _____
    * _____
    * _____

99. Did you learn about financial
    planning/money
    management?
    * _____
    * _____
    * _____

> ### Thoughts to Consider
>
> *"Day by day, WHAT you choose, WHAT you think and WHAT you do is WHO you become."*
>
> *-Heraclitus*

100. Do you see yourself professionally in 5 years?
    * _____
    * _____
    * _____

W

BONUS QUESTION…

101. Can you define in simple words, WHO you are, WHAT you do, WHEN you did it, WHY you do it, and WHERE it is done?

* _____
* _____
* _____
* _____
* _____

> **Thoughts to Consider**
>
> *"Every great dream begins with a dreamer, always remember you have with you the strength, the patience, and the passion to reach for the stars and change the world."*
>
> *-Harriet Tubman*

"You can go wherever you want in this world. But one thing is for certain, you cannot escape how you view yourself."

-Norwegian Proverb

A Case in Point: WHERE I Want to Be

Michael was born and raised in an inner-city urban community. The neighborhood WHERE he grew up was surrounded by drugs, gangs, and violence. Each night, his family would be startled by the sounds of gunshots and sirens from emergency first responders (e.g. firetrucks, ambulances, etc.). Occasionally, the swooping sounds of policing helicopters would circulate the friendly skies like craving vultures searching for a runaway outlaw.

Michael is a high-school senior. He was an All American Athlete for two consecutive years with the hopes of one day playing with a professional football team. Unfortunately, doing a scrimmage football game, he suffered a permanent knee injury that derailed his future career plans of playing as a professional athlete. However, Michael was determined to beat the odds; and although he has faced many trials and tribulations, his level of perseverance and positive attitude provided a new outlook on life.

During a high-school field trip to several colleges and universities, he was introduced to the profession of kinesiology. Realizing that things don't always turn out as planned, Michael met with several admissions counselors before deciding to pursue the field of sports medicine.

After graduating from high-school and successfully completing all the prerequisite course requirements at a local university, he was later admitted into a Doctor of Physical Therapy (DPT) program. While enrolled as a full-time student, he began volunteering as a youth football coach at a community outreach center. In fact, he was honored by several city officials for implementing an afterschool athletic program to support children raised in underserved neighborhoods.

Upon finishing the DPT program, he was later offered a job working with a professional football team as a physical therapist. In his spare time, he continued to volunteer at the local community center as an athletic coach. Michael is a true testament to all the possible places WHERE you can go if you put your heart and mind to being all that you can be.

A Case in Point: WHERE Did the Time Go

It was 4:55PM and close to quitting time. Becky turned off her computer and started packing up her belongings while dreading the 45-minute drive home. Everybody knows that the rush hour traffic at 5:00 PM can be a challenge to navigate. Despite the long drive, Becky has found a way to occupy her time by listening to podcasts on self-improvement and leadership concepts.

For the past fifteen years, she has traveled the same route back and forth to work. A lot has changed since she started working as an office clerk at the community hospital. New employees and supervisors have come and gone. Even the technology has changed. Needless to say, it seems as if every process or personal need can be solved by a downloadable application for purchase. Apparently, the days of getting a cup of coffee at the local café is of the past. You can now have it delivered to your desk within 10-minutes or less.

Over the past two months, Becky has not been quite herself. Her colleagues have noticed a change in her attitude and work productivity. She has frequently complained of feeling extremely fatigued, restless, and depressed. In addition, she has taken sick leave from work at least five days within the past two weeks. Eventually Beck was referred to an employee help hotline in which a mental health specialist was assigned to assist her. After several private sessions, the therapist suggested Becky revisit her life's goals and set realistic expectations. Each day, Becky has witnessed time slowly passing her by without making any life changes. Her dreams of becoming an executive administrative assistant seemed to be fading fast. She no longer has the desire or motivation to work in her current role as a clerk. Neither does she have any vacation or sick time available to use. With very few options for consideration, Becky scheduled an appointment with the Human Resources Department to discuss her retirement options.

The good news is she qualifies for early departure. Unfortunately, if she elects to do so, she will not be eligible to receive full health benefits. After contemplating for several days on the available choices, Becky decided to take an early retirement. During an exit interview with the human resource office manager she emotionally stated, "After 25-years of service to this organization, my only regret is I never actualized my goals of becoming an executive assistant. I wish I would have at least tried......"

Questions for Discussion:

- Based on the two case studies you have read, can you reflect on each person's story and identify any similarities or differences?

- Do you possess any characteristics similar to the persons identified in the story? Why or Why not?

- Do you see yourself falling into either of their situations? If so, explain how?

A Simple Exercise

WHERE you are positioned in life today may differ from WHERE you were five (5) years ago. In the boxes provided below, document three (3) areas of your life WHERE you have seen the most personal growth. Exactly WHAT did it take for you arrive WHERE you are?

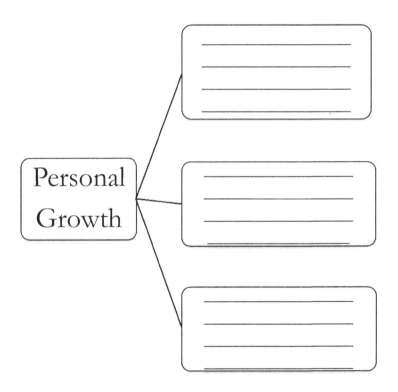

Personal Goals

In the spaces provided below, list three (3) personal goals related the question "**WHERE**" that you would like to achieve within the next twelve (12) months. Evaluate your progress by checking the met or unmet boxes at the end of a four (4) month period. If you did not meet your goal(s), document your plan to reassess and accomplish your objective(s).

Date:	4 Months			
Goal	Met	Unmet	Plan	
1.				
2.				
3.				
Notes:				
Date:	8 Months			
Goal	Met	Unmet	Plan	
1.				
2.				
3.				
Notes:				
Date:	12 Months			
Goal	Met	Unmet	Plan	
1.				
2.				
3.				
Notes:				

W

Time to Reflect

Now that you have completed the questions, simple exercise, personal goals log, and read the case scenarios, please take time to reflect on the queries that you had most difficulty responding to. Self-reflection begins with you taking time to look in the mirror and acknowledge your areas of improvement and strengths. If you struggled with answering three (3) or more of the questions, perhaps spending more time exploring your responses is needed. Once you have successfully answered all of the questions, document your thoughts in the self-reflection section.

SELF-REFLECTION

SELF-REFLECTION

_____

_____

_____

_____

_____

_____

_____

_____

_____

_____

_____

_____

_____

_____

_____

_____

_____

_____

_____

_____

SELF-REFLECTION

W

Final Thoughts

Great leaders are aware that success is a process. By taking personal inventory of your strengths and areas of improvement, you will find yourself becoming more focused and motivated toward goal attainment. Everyone one has the potential to be a great leader; however are you inspired enough to do the things that are necessary to bring your vision unto fruition?

Now that you've had the opportunity to explore the 101 questions that every leader should know on their journey to success (i.e. WHO, WHAT, WHY, WHEN, and WHERE), the final questions to answer are focused on HOW, which I refer to as the H-Factors. For many people that master the 5W questions, the struggle remains with HOW. Exactly HOW do you make your hopes and dreams become a reality?

The H-Factors are highlighted in the sequel to The Essentials of Success. If you enjoyed reading this book, I'm certain you will like the sequel as well. The questions provided throughout the book will not only challenge your thought processes, but also your methods of preparation, creativity, and strategies to success.

W

About The Author

Joseph Morris has spent over 20-years in various leadership roles ranging from clinical practice and academia, to executive leadership in corporate America. His ability to take complex leadership topics such as organizational governance, team building, and self-improvement and explain it in practical terms has earned him various distinguished awards and recognitions. He is often referred to as "A Maverick of Change." Joseph has earned several professional degrees including a Bachelors and Masters of Science in Nursing (MSN) from University of Michigan and a Doctor of Philosophy (PhD) from University of Los Angeles, California (UCLA). In his spare time he enjoys public speaking, mentoring, and creative writing.

Questions regarding this book or to contact the author please email essentials.of.success@gmail.com

> "We all have different journeys in life. And everyone has a particular role to play. But the answers to most of the questions surrounding success rest within the Who, What, Why, When, and Where."

-Dr. Joseph Morris

Made in the USA
Monee, IL
10 August 2022